Louise L. Hay

Colors
&
Numbers
1996

HAY HOUSE, INC.
Carson, CA

Hay House, Inc.
1154 E. Dominguez St.
P.O. Box 6204
Carson, CA 90749-6204

First Hay House edition published 1987.

Tenth edition, 1995.

ISBN 1-56170-123-8

To all the colorful beings on this beautiful planet. You are beautiful and so am I. Let us love and appreciate the uniqueness of ourselves and each other. We now fill our days with color and joy.

BOOKS, AUDIOS, AND VIDEOS BY LOUISE L. HAY

Books

The Aids Book: Creating a Positive Approach
Colors & Numbers
A Garden of Thoughts: My Affirmation Journal
Heal Your Body
Heart Thoughts: A Treasury of Inner Wisdom
Life! Reflections on Your Journey
Love Your Body
Love Yourself, Heal Your Life Workbook
Loving Thoughts for Health and Healing
Loving Thoughts for Increasing Prosperity
Loving Thoughts for Loving Yourself
Loving Thoughts for a Perfect Day
Meditations to Heal Your Life
101 Power Thoughts
The Power Is Within You
You Can Heal Your Life

Coloring Books/Audiocassettes for Children

Lulu and the Ant: A Message of Love
Lulu and the Dark: Conquering Fears
Lulu and Willy the Duck: Learning Mirror Work

Audiocassettes

Aids: A Positive Approach
Cancer: Discovering Your Healing Power
Feeling Fine Affirmations
Gift of the Present with Joshua Leeds
Heal Your Body (Book-on-Tape)
Love Your Body (Book-on-Tape)
Loving Yourself
Meditations for Personal Healing
Meditations to Heal Your Life

Morning and Evening Meditations
Overcoming Fears
The Power Is Within You (Book-on-Tape)
Self Healing
Songs of Affirmation with Joshua Leeds
What I Believe/Deep Relaxation
You Can Heal Your Life Study Course
You Can Heal Your Life (Book-on-Tape)

Conversations on Living Lecture Series

Change and Transition
Dissolving Barriers
The Forgotten Child Within
How to Love Yourself
The Power of Your Spoken Word
Receiving Prosperity
Totality of Possibilities
Your Thoughts Create Your Life

Personal Power Through Imagery Series

Anger Releasing
Forgiveness/Loving the Inner Child

Subliminal Mastery Series

Feeling Fine Affirmations
Love Your Body Affirmations
Safe Driving Affirmations
Self-Esteem Affirmations
Self-Healing Affirmations
Stress-Free Affirmations

Videocassettes

Dissolving Barriers
Doors Opening: A Positive Approach to Aids
Receiving Prosperity
You Can Heal Your Life Study Course
Your Thoughts Create Your Life

Available at your local bookstore, or call: (800) 654-5126

Table of Contents

Foreword

This book provides a fun way to associate colors, numbers, affirmations, and spiritual ideals in your daily life. There are many schools of thought on the matter of significance of numbers, and *Colors & Numbers* among them is worthy of your contemplation. What I find especially valuable is the way that Louise Hay utilizes affirmations to set the mood for the day. I enjoyed the pleasurable, constructive, and refreshing approach. Read this book and enjoy your numerous days.

Christopher Gibson
Metaphysical Lecturer and Counselor
Santa Monica, California

Colors & Numbers at a Glance

Number	Color(s)	Gems	Key Word
1	red	ruby	beginnings
2	orange	moonstone	cooperate
3	yellow	topaz	enjoyment
4	green	emerald/jade	practical
5	blue	turquoise/aquamarine	change
6	indigo (navy blue)	pear/sapphire/lapis	responsibility
7	purple/violet	amethyst	faith
8	beige/brown/pink	diamond	achievement
9	all pastels	opals/gold	completion
11/2	black/white or pearl gray	silver	intuition
22/4	coral/russet	coral/copper	greatness

Colors & Numbers

The study of color is fascinating. We are surrounded by color at all times. Even the so-called colorless has color. A world without color is hard to imagine.

When we think of color, nature may first come to mind. We look forward to the first soft green that confirms spring is on its way. To see crocuses and daffodils burst out of the thawing ground warms our hearts. The developing of the full lush green and colors of mid-summer enables us to feel the abundance of the earth. Then comes the breathtaking autumn spectacle of the yellows, oranges, and reds. When they are gone, winter moves in with its quiet white blanket of snow and the gray trunks and branches of the trees. We await spring once more.

How many times have we watched a sunset or a sunrise and marveled at the incredible colors? Sunrise on the desert is an awe-filled experience. From early dawn to midday to dusk to midnight, there are thousands of gradations of light and color. When we take time to look up to the blue of the sky, we feel the tranquility and peace of the open expanse of space. Colors no longer merely serve as a decorative or ornamental function. They affect us in deeper ways.

Color is an essential part of our lives. Yet most of us remain largely ignorant of the benefit to be gained from our conscious use of color. Each color vibrates with its own energy, which we can use to enhance our lives.

The study of numbers is ancient and respected. Pythagoras, the Greek philosopher, who is often considered to be the father of numerology, felt "numbers to be the ultimate elements of the universe." Even as late as the Renaissance, churches were constructed using mystical number systems that the architects believed enhanced an experience of God while within their walls.

Colors and numbers both have significance. In this book they are used together, as numerology teaches us that each number has an associated color, and that each month, each day, the vibrations change, and as the number vibrations change, so do the colors.

There are so many ways we can cooperate with Life. Consciously using our personal numbers and colors is one way for our days to flow smoother. This book shows us yet another way to integrate colors and numbers into our daily living practices and bring them into balance. Numbers and colors fill our days, and they are useful to our lives and attitudes. They may form a basis of our affirmations and our declarations of ourselves, which is exactly the purpose of this book.

Everything seems to be numbered. Streets and houses and telephones and bank accounts are all numbered.

Every appliance and electrical gadget is numbered. So are holidays and calendars and Social Security cards and credit cards and paper money. But the most personal numbers we have are our own ages and our birthday numbers.

Color is also everywhere in our lives. We all eat food, we wear clothing, and many of us wear jewels and gemstones. We color our rooms and our furniture. Our mode of transportation is colored, as is our place of business. When we consciously choose colors and gems and foods and clothing that blend with our own personal vibratory rates on a daily basis, we enhance our ability to flow with the currents of life. Health and our healthy attitude toward ourselves may be stated by the colors we wear.

Men and women, young and elderly, active or sedentary will find meaning by assimilating colors and numbers into their lives. Whatever your lifestyle may be, no matter where you may live, the use of color in your life is constant—and numbers are everywhere.

All colors are good, and we feel more comfortable with certain colors at certain times. Our day-to-day living can be enhanced by surrounding ourselves with the colors that are most harmonious with our own personal vibrations for that day. It is the study of numbers that reveals our daily, monthly, and yearly vibrations. When we choose the color that is associated with those particular vibrations and pay attention to what that number is telling us, we are more in tune with Life.

As you will see, each PERSONAL DAY has a color that vibrates with the number of that day. Each PERSONAL

DAY also has a jewel that resonates to the color and number. Gems, like colors, have vibrations that, if worn, can enhance a desired mood. There is also a key phrase that sets the tone for this PERSONAL DAY.

I have added an affirmation for each PERSONAL DAY. I encourage you to concentrate on these positive ideas. I like saying them in the morning shortly after I wake up, preparing for a fresh, new, learning, growing, and fun-filled day.

We each have our own personal number vibrations and personal color vibrations. Some of these numbers, like our birthdate, are permanent. We also have temporary personal colors as the calendar changes. By consciously surrounding ourselves with our personal colors, we become more in tune with the cosmic forces.

There are many good books available if you wish to pursue this subject in depth. I list a few titles in the bibliography at the end of this book. For now, let us explore one aspect of the study of numbers as applied to the use of color in our daily lives. In the next section, I explain the methods used to find your own PERSONAL YEAR vibration, your PERSONAL MONTH vibration, and your PERSONAL DAY vibration.

Calculating Your Personal Year, Month, and Day

First, there is a Universal Year (the current year) vibration. This vibration is in operation for everyone. We find the number that corresponds with it by adding the four digits of the current year. For instance, the year 1996 is figured by adding $1 + 9 + 9 + 6 = 25$. In numerology, we continue reducing numbers until we have a single digit; therefore, we add $2 + 5 = 7$, which shows us that 1996 is a #7 Universal Year.

PERSONAL YEAR

Use the space above to discover your PERSONAL YEAR VIBRATION. Add your own BIRTH MONTH AND BIRTH DAY to the current UNIVERSAL YEAR.

If your birthday is October 23, you add:

10 (for October)
23 (for the day)
7 (for the Universal Year, 1996)
___
40 4 + 0 = 4

1996 = #4 PERSONAL YEAR

PERSONAL MONTH

To find your PERSONAL MONTH VIBRATION for the current month, add your PERSONAL YEAR to the calendar month. Using the above as an example, if your PERSONAL YEAR is a #4 and it is currently the month of April, you would calculate as follows: #4 (Personal Year) + 4 (April) = 8. (Remember, reduce double-digit numbers to a single digit.) Your PERSONAL MONTH VIBRATION would be #8.

4 (for Personal Year as above)
4 (for Calendar Month, April)
___
8

April 1996 = #8 PERSONAL MONTH

PERSONAL DAY

To find your PERSONAL DAY VIBRATION, add your PER-
SONAL MONTH to the calendar day.

Using the above example of April 1996, if this were a #8
PERSONAL MONTH for you, and today is April 1, add the
PERSONAL MONTH number to the calendar day:

For April 1, 1996, add:

8   (for Personal Month as above)
1   (for Calendar Day, April 1)
___
9

April 1, 1996 = #9 PERSONAL DAY

Once you have determined your Personal Day, then each day follows in numerical sequence, from #1 to #9. After a #9 Personal Day, you will move to a #1 Personal Day. This same procedure will follow for the remainder of the month. When you enter a new Personal Month, you begin your calculations again.

We provide a date calendar in this book, so you may calculate your personal numbers for the rest of the year. It is much easier to do them all at once, so your numbers are ready for you as you need them. You may place this book near your closet or bathroom, so you can easily refer to it each morning before dressing.

If your calculations for your Personal vibrations total an 11 or 22, do not reduce these numbers to a 2 or 4. The numbers 11 and 22 are considered Master Numbers. They indicate that you are being given an opportunity to operate for that period on a higher vibration. You are more in tune at this time with higher, more universal principles operating in your world and in the world as a whole. Write them as "11/2" or "22/4" so that you are reminded that you have a choice of being the 2 or reaching up to the 11, or a 4 reaching for 22. For instance, the 2 follows a leader; the 11 is the leader. The 4 works for the self; the 22 works for the community.

A good thing to know is that whatever the Personal Year, the first Personal Month will be the next number. For instance, January of a #8 Personal Year will be a #9 Personal Month. The 1st day of a #9 Personal Month will be a #1 Personal Day.

DOUBLE AND TRIPLE INTENSITY DAYS

The Personal Day numbers of the 9th, 18th, and 27th of each calendar month will be the same numbers as the number of the Personal Month. For example, in a #6 Personal Month, the 9th, 18th, and 27th will all be #6 Personal Days. These are DOUBLE INTENSITY Days, which you may wish to star in your calendar. On Double Intensity days, the energy surrounding the specific indications will be intensified doubly, meaning that you have an even greater opportunity to utilize these energies for your benefit and growth.

September is always a special month. The number of the month of September is always the same number as the number of your Personal Year. Therefore, the 9th, 18th, and 27th of September are always TRIPLE INTENSITY. For instance, in a #6 Personal Year, September will be a #6 Personal Month for you; therefore, the entire month will be intensified. In September, the 9th, 18th, and 27th will also be #6, Personal Days of TRIPLE INTENSITY. You may star these days in your calendar, also, perhaps with a different colored pen, to indicate that the energies will be tripled on these days.

HELPFUL HINTS

The last two months of a calendar year are always the same Personal Number months as the beginning two months of the next calendar year. However, the yearly personal vibrations will be different. In a #6 Personal Year, November will be a #8 Personal Month, and December will be a #9 Personal Month. In the following two months of the next calendar year (which will be your #7 Personal Year), January will be a #8 Personal Month, and February will be a #9 Personal Month. The numbers will be the same, but the yearly personal vibrations will be different, as you will now be in a #7 Personal Year.

Of course, you can do anything on any day; however, if you take advantage of the specific energy which that day presents, you will feel more in harmony with life. If it is snowing, it is not in your best interest to go out in shorts and bare feet. Your day would be more comfortable if you wore clothing that was appropriate for snow. And so it is with life. There are times when certain behaviors and activities are more appropriate and comfortable than others. Some days it just feels RIGHT to go shopping or to do your banking — or it may feel RIGHT to scrub your floors. You are keying into the energies that surround you and your life at all times. This book presents a way to specifically tap into them.

In numerology, black is seldom used. On a 1-1/2 day, black may be worn if it is combined with white. Though I always feel pearl gray and silver are more nourishing colors to wear on those days. Black is the absence of color, and in many years of counseling, I found that people who wore a lot of black, or who wore black all the time, were seldom happy people. Black has a tendency to confine and repress the spirit. If you have an emotional problem and/or wear black frequently, I would suggest that you stay away from it for a month and see if you do not become more cheerful. You may even find more fun in life!

If you're using these ideas for the first time, it may take you a while to develop a wardrobe that incorporates all the colors in clothing for each season. In the meantime, use whatever you have on hand. It doesn't have to be a whole outfit. A scarf, or a belt, or a handkerchief — or even colorful underwear — will do nicely. Sometimes it's just carrying a colored pen or even putting a few flowers in a vase to remind us of the color vibration for the day. Give a loved one or friend a gift in his or her own Personal Day color.

The food we eat is also colorful. Therefore, the colors we take into our bodies in the form of food are as meaningful as the colors we wear and with which we surround ourselves. For instance, on a red #1 Personal Day, red apples, tomatoes, or beets might attract and nourish us. (Refer to the food-color chart on page 53 for other ideas.)

As you enter a new Personal Year, you could buy something for the house that will reflect this color all year long. You might purchase a new bedspread, or paint your favorite room in a pleasing shade of your Personal Year color. Perhaps you might buy yourself a ring or a pendant. If you are ready to buy a new car, your Personal Year vibration could influence the color you choose. Use your imagination to bring meaningful color into your life. Your imagination is reflective of your image of yourself and the love you are developing for yourself.

When in doubt — if you don't have the appropriate color at hand for your Personal Day — you can always use the color for your Personal Month or Personal Year. The number and color of your Personal Year is like background music for everything you will do that year.

Try it, it's fun! See what happens.

Using Your Numbers

Now that you have calculated your own current Personal Year, Month, and Day, turn to the section that explains your Personal Year. Read the indications for your Personal Year and what this year means for you. The Personal Year is the background music for your Personal Day. Each day when you arise, turn to the number section that corresponds to the number for your Personal Day. Then, meditate on the concepts and affirmations I have presented that will help you to achieve the most good from your Personal Day.

The indications for the Personal Day are to be used in conjunction with the Personal Month and Personal Year. The indications for the Personal Month are the same as the Personal Year of the same number, so you will turn to the section on Personal Year to find the indications for your Personal Month. I prefer to concentrate on TODAY, and therefore utilize the indications for the Personal Day and Personal Year more than for the Personal Month.

Personal Year

#1
Personal Year

Color
RED

Jewel
RUBY

Key Word
BEGINNINGS

This is the year for new beginnings, for new starts, for new ideas, for anything new. It is a time to plant, to sow seeds. Seeds planted this year will have an effect on the next eight years. Remember, seeds do not come up overnight. They must first germinate and take root. Only then do they grow. Give your ideas a chance to take root. Develop a plan for what you want in this nine-year cycle, and begin to work on it now. Be yourself, and push forward with determination. Take control. Look to yourself rather than to partnerships or unions. During this time period, independence and self-promotion have a strong influence. Lay your groundwork now. Stay busy and keep things moving. This is your year to pioneer and break new ground.

"I BREAK NEW GROUND AND BEGIN NEW VENTURES!"

#2
Personal Year

Color
ORANGE

Jewel
MOONSTONE

Key Word
PATIENCE

The seeds you planted last year are under the ground ready to germinate. This year you deserve some rest and quiet. Make sure that you have it. Study and acquire knowledge. Practice diplomacy and tact. Sharing and teamwork are best. Be very cooperative. Do not force anything this year. Be patient and wait. That which is right for you will come to you. Pay attention to details. Collect what you need. Look behind the scenes. The opportunity is on the way. Think and plan and be peaceful. Stay calm and wait. Love is favored. This is a very good year for relationships and partnerships.

"I TRUST THE PROCESS OF LIFE TO UNFOLD IN DIVINE RIGHT ORDER!"

#3
Personal Year

Color
YELLOW

Jewel
TOPAZ

Key Word
ENJOYMENT

This is your year for fun. That which you started two years ago is now beginning to come to life. Believe in yourself. The seeds are beginning to send out roots. The birth is evident. All is well, and you feel it. Love is everywhere. It's a time for friends and doing things you enjoy. Entertain and go to parties and gatherings. Go on vacations and holidays. The influence this year is social and artistic. Express yourself creatively as much as possible. Laugh and smile and sing and dance and spread sunshine all around you. Your year will be full of joy.

"I LOVE LIFE AND THE JOY OF LIVING!"

#4
Personal Year

Color
GREEN

Jewels
EMERALD/JADE

Key Word
PRACTICAL

Now it's time to get back to work. The seeds are sending shoots up through the ground. Do your weeding. Be productive and organized. Build your foundation. Be busy and follow your schedule. Take inventory. Get your life in order and attend to the details. Use self-discipline and avoid being lazy. Do things cheerfully, and you will have all the energy you need. Take good care of your health. You are building for the future, so be constructive. Solve the problems this year. The more effort you give, the more rewards you will reap. Everything will turn out well.

"I TURN EVERYTHING INTO OPPORTUNITY!"

#5
Personal Year

Color
BLUE

Jewels
TURQUOISE/AQUAMARINE

Key Word
CHANGE

Freedom and change are in the air. The crop is growing. After all your work last year, you deserve a vacation. Let this be your year to dress up. Put your best foot forward. Drop the routine. Discard old ideas. Do something unusual. Be different this year. Get out and experience life in a new way. A great year to learn a new language or experience life in a new place. Make changes—in yourself, your home, your lifestyle, your business. Make sure these changes benefit others, too. See as many people as you can. Look for good surprises. Yet, don't throw all caution to the wind. Keep active, not restless. This can be a very satisfying year.

"I WELCOME CHANGE AND EXPAND MY BOUNDARIES!"

#6
Personal Year

Color
INDIGO (navy blue)

Jewels
PEARL/SAPPHIRE/LAPIS

Key Word
RESPONSIBILITY

Now it's time for home and family, groups and friends. The plants are flowering. Make your home the center of your life. Be responsible, fair, and just. Be of service, and accept your duties willingly. Take care of all your personal belongings, people, places, and things. This year is the best of all for marriage. It's the perfect year to move into a new home. Make music a big part of your life. Do all your entertaining at home. Set your standards and keep them. Complete whatever you start. Have a rhythm and harmony in your life. Anything you do for the benefit of the group is good. Be the counselor. Give assistance whenever it is needed. It's your year to give to yourself. A deeply satisfying year.

"I ACCEPT MY RESPONSIBILITIES WITH LOVE AND JOY!"

#7
Personal Year

Colors
PURPLE/VIOLET

Jewel
AMETHYST

Key Word
FAITH

This is an inner year. The fruit is just beginning to show on the vine, and we must have faith it will ripen. Take time for reflection, study, and self-analysis. Spend lots of time alone, and use it constructively. Analyze your thoughts and actions. What would you like to change about yourself? The number 7 always reveals things we normally do not see. Look over your life. This year is for inner growth and preparation. Don't reach out or try to force things; let things come to you. Release the business world as much as possible. Meditate, be introspective. Leave the social life for another time. You may travel to learn more about yourself. This is a spiritual year, so flow with it. Allow your soul to grow.

"I ENJOY THE INNER QUEST AND FIND MANY ANSWERS!"

#8
Personal Year

Colors
BEIGE/BROWN/PINK

Jewel
DIAMOND

Key Word
ACHIEVEMENT

This is the success year. It's harvest time. That which you began eight years ago is now ready. Take your product to the market. Business and all material things are yours now. Put out some effort, and you will accomplish a lot. Go after what you want. Be the executive, the manager, the organizer. Be efficient and businesslike. Be self-confident. Be honest and fair in all your dealings. You can accomplish big things. Look for unexpected money. Business trips are favored. This is your year to achieve. Go for it!

"I AM THE PROSPEROUS, SUCCESSFUL EXECUTIVE OF MY WORLD!"

#9
Personal Year

Colors
ALL PASTELS

Jewels
OPALS/GOLD

Key Word
COMPLETION

It's a time for completion and fulfillment. The garden is finished for this cycle, yet some of the crops continue to produce. This is the year of spring-cleaning. Get into the corners. Review everything and toss out al that is no longer useful in your life—people, places, ideas, and things. If it's finished, let it go. Don't hang on. Many things will pass out of your life this year. Bless them and release them. You are making room for the new next year. There is much happiness around you. This is a year for endings. Do not begin new things. Don't look for new personal love affairs now; they won't last. Enjoy the artistic part of life. Take a long trip and learn about others. Give away. Give to others. Be tolerant, compassionate, and forgiving. Love must be shared with all. Really understand the kinship of everyone on this planet. The old cycle closes. Make ready for the new one next year.

"I AM SATISFIED AND FULFILLED AND COMPLETE!"

#11/2
Personal Year

Colors
BLACK/WHITE or PEARL GRAY

Jewel
SILVER

Key Word
INTUITION

11/2 is a Master Number. Rise above daily routine. Shine like a star. Set new standards for yourself on the internal level. Do more investigating on the spiritual and meta-physical side of life. Universal love is more important than personal love this year. Keep your own inner peace, no matter what. The occult will have more interest for you. This is not a business year, although you will have lots of good ideas for later. Live up to your ideals. Prepare yourself. Fame and honor could come to you this year. Now is a time for inner growth, illumination, and reflection.

"I LISTEN TO THE INNER VOICE OF WISDOM!"

#22/4
Personal Year

Colors
CORAL/RUSSET

Jewels
CORAL/COPPER

Key Word
GREATNESS

22/4 is a Master Number. Superior accomplishments can be achieved if you rise above the 4. The community needs you. If you work only for yourself, you will miss the full advantage of the year. If you work on big plans for the good of many, then your projects will be successful. This is an opportunity for a power year involving big projects. Build something worthwhile. Use all your mental powers. You don't get a year like this often. Prominence and power can be yours.

"I WORK FOR THE GOOD OF THE PLANET, AND I AM BLESSED!"

Personal Day

#1
Personal Day

Color	Jewel
RED	RUBY

TIME TO BEGIN

Be independent. Do what you want to do. Go after things. Go to new places. Meet new people. Try out new ideas. Begin a new job. Be active. Great for a first date. You will find that men are important in your life today. Be the leader today. Trust yourself and your intuition. Be original and creative. Be ambitious. Feel your own power. Be courageous. Anger, stubbornness, impatience, or worry may tend to undermine your abilities. Look for the new.

"I OPEN NEW DOORS TO LIFE!"

Today I trust the Infinite Wisdom within me to lead me and guide me in new areas of living. I am safe and secure as I step out, trusting the Process of Life to be there for me. Life supports me every step of the way. I am fed, clothed, and housed and loved in ways that are deeply fulfilling to me. I meet the new with open arms, knowing that it will soon become familiar. Knowing that all friends and lovers were once strangers to me, I welcome new people into my life. Today is a glorious new day for me.

#2
Personal Day

Color	Jewel
ORANGE	MOONSTONE

COOPERATE

Be peaceful. A time to agree with others. Do more than your share. Be patient, tolerant, and diplomatic. It's time to be receptive. Collect that which you need. Look for that antique. Observe, listen, and think. Put others at ease, and be aware of their feelings. Create harmony. Enjoy your women friends. Relax, be gentle and pleasant. Wait.

"I AM KIND AND CONSIDERATE OF OTHERS!"

Yesterday I planted in the Garden of Life. Today I patiently wait for the seeds to awaken. I have time and consideration for everyone around me. I joyfully help wherever I can, easing the load of others. That which I give out returns to me multiplied. I gather to myself that which I need for the future. This is a harmonious, receptive, loving, peaceful day.

#3
Personal Day

Color
YELLOW

Jewel
TOPAZ

IT'S PARTY TIME

Laugh, have fun. All people are important. It's a social day. Sing, dance, and play. Express yourself. Love everybody. Today is truly the joy of living. Look beautiful. Feel handsome. Experience the joy that is in you, and radiate it all around you. Bless everyone and everything. Make others smile. Let your creativity express itself freely. The best day for shopping. It's a people day. Love them all.

"I RADIATE JOY AND SHARE IT WITH OTHERS!"

Joy flows through my veins and is expressed in every part of my being. I know my seeds are sprouting, and it is a time for rejoicing. I am joyously exuberant and in harmony with all of life. My life is a party to be experienced and shared with everyone I know. My creativity flows, and I give of it freely. I am beautiful, and everybody loves me. All is well in my world, and I share this feeling with others.

#4
Personal Day

Color	**Jewels**
GREEN	EMERALD/JADE

TIME TO WORK

It's time to get up early. Get those chores done. You have lots of energy today. Get going on those projects. Pay your bills. Write those letters. Balance the budget. Clean the house. Wash the car. Be organized and dependable. Do your repairs. The work you do today is lasting. Have a health checkup. Get things ready for tomorrow.

"I AM ORGANIZED AND PRODUCTIVE!"

The first tender shoots are coming through the ground, and there is work to do. I joyfully pull the weeds of negativity from within my consciousness. The Power of the Universe backs me in this endeavor, and I have boundless energy. I get things done easily and quickly. I build firm foundations for tomorrow. I am healthy in body, mind, and spirit.

#5
Personal Day

Color
BLUE

Jewels
TURQUOISE/AQUAMARINE

CHANGE AND SURPRISE

Look your best. Really dress up. Get out and look for the new. Positive change is in the air. Today you are free. Expect a good surprise. Do something different. Be flexible. Change your routine. Promote and advertise yourself or your products. Look at another side of life. Give something away. Sell something. The best day for haircuts or surgery. You feel free today.

"I WELCOME CHANGE AND REJOICE IN THE NEW!"

The crop is growing well and takes care of itself, soaking in the sunshine of life and the nourishment of the soil. I am free to allow the different experiences of life to come in. I am alert to a wonderful, positive surprise that benefits me in a delightful way. I look terrific and feel terrific. Here I am, World, open and receptive to all good, which I accept with joy and pleasure and gratitude.

#6
Personal Day

ADJUSTMENT TIME

Take a personal inventory. Look at your house. Could you make it more comfortable? How about yourself? Could you be more polished? Review your diet. Does it need adjusting? Look at your personality. Could it be more cheerful? Look at your responsibilities. Any that need taking care of? Are you sticking your nose into other people's business? If so, let go. Do you owe anything? Now is the time to pay up. Stay home. Enjoy your family. Entertain at home. Fill your day with music. If possible, do not travel. Save creative writing for another day. Teachers excel, group work is favored. A wonderful day for moving into a new home.

"MY HOME IS A PEACEFUL HAVEN!"

My plants are in bloom and are a joy and a beauty to behold. They enhance my home, and I tend to them carefully. It is a duty I enjoy. I am responsible. Where needed, I easily make adjustments to my home. It is a comfortable place to be—for me and for others. I open my home and welcome guests with music and love. They are like a loving family to me.

31

#7
Personal Day

Colors
PURPLE/VIOLET

Jewel
AMETHYST

LOOK WITHIN

Be alone, at least for part of the day. Be still. Read. Think. Listen to your inner soul. Drop the business world. If you pursue money today, it will run from you. If you keep still and wait, things will come to you. Study something spiritual or scientific. If you read the scriptures, choose Matthew 6 on this day. Work with your plants. Take a long walk or a drive in the country. The number 7 always reveals something. Meditate. Be open.

"I LOOK WITHIN AND RECEIVE ANSWERS!"

The fruit is small, yet I have faith that the Universe is in the process of producing an enormous crop for me. So silently I take time to go within, to be in touch with my own inner wisdom. I look with love at nature and all her beauty, and I am renewed and refreshed. I trust Life to take care of me. I know that whatever I need will always be there for me. The Power that supplies my breath will supply all else just as easily and freely.

#8
Personal Day

Colors
BEIGE/BROWN/PINK

Jewel
DIAMOND

SUCCESSFUL BUSINESS

Ambition stirs within you. It's a time for advancement. Look and act successful. A big business day. Be an executive. Organize and reorganize. Use good judgment. Pay your bills. Do all your financial and legal work. Best day for signing leases or contracts. Go to the gym or have a health checkup. You often receive unexpected money. Help someone less fortunate. Success is already yours now.

"I AM POWERFUL AND PROSPEROUS!"

The bountiful harvest is in and ready for the market-place. I am the executive of my life and affairs. I have innate good judgment, for I am connected at all times to the Universal Intelligence. With the Universe as my partner, I go from success to success. I am the benevolent and loving director of the kingdom I have created. The more I help others, the more I prosper and grow. Where I am, everybody wins.

#9
Personal Day

Colors	**Jewels**
ALL PASTELS	OPALS and GOLD

HUMANITY

All the world is your family. Be a humanitarian. Help everyone you can. Give something away. Be generous and kind. No beginnings today; finish up things. Go for completion. Never for a first date—it won't last. No shopping unless it's for a gift. Clean out closets and drawers. If you don't use something you own, give it away or sell it. Release all that no longer benefits you—things, ideas, habits, relationships. Be an artist. Use your creative talents. A great day for a public performance. What you give out will come back to you, so give only the best. Close the chapter; tomorrow you start anew.

"I AM ONE WITH ALL OF LIFE. THE WHOLE WORLD IS MY FAMILY!"

The work is done, the cycle is complete. Everything is clean. I release and let go; I gladly give away all that I no longer need. I am generous with the fellow travelers on this planet, for they are my brothers and sisters. I forgive and forget. I am free. I give freely of my heart and possessions. I have understanding, and fulfillment is mine, and I am deeply satisfied. All is well in my world.

#11/2
Personal Day

Colors
BLACK/WHITE or PEARL GRAY

Jewel
SILVER

FOLLOW YOUR STAR

11/2 is a Master Number. Leave commercialism behind you. The vibrations today are highly attuned and very spiritual. Your intuition is strong. Do not force anything. Be silent. Keep the peace. Let the day flow and be on time. Do not read. Go within. Don't argue; you won't win. It's not your fault anyway. Be the light of the world for the world. You can be greatly inspired today, or you can inspire others.

"I FOLLOW MY INNER STAR!"

I have a direct pipeline of wisdom and knowledge from the highest source. As I turn within, all the answers I seek are there for the finding. Every question I have is easily answered by my own inspiration. I inspire others. I am a shining example of love and light. Today I sparkle and shine in a quiet and peaceful way.

#22/4
Personal Day

Colors
CORAL or RUSSET

Jewels
CORAL and COPPER

GIVE OF YOURSELF

22/4 is a Master Number. Forget yourself and your own interests. Whatever you do today must be for the good of all. Work for the community or for the world. Any plans you make must be large and for the highest interests of all. Benefit others. It will bring you good fortune.

"I JOYFULLY BLESS AND PROSPER EVERYONE!"

It is my joy and pleasure to share all that I have and all that I am with everyone on the planet. I give freely of my talents and abilities and resources. My viewpoint is ever larger, and I work for the highest interests of all concerned. I am one with the Universe now and forevermore.

YOUR PERSONAL CALENDAR

EXAMPLE: *If* September is your #2 Personal Month, then October will be your #3 Personal Month...

	SUN	MON	TUES	WED	THURS	FRI	SAT	
1996 **S E P T E M B E R**	3¹	4²	5³	6⁴	7⁵	8⁶	9⁷	**YOUR PERSONAL MONTH** #2
	1⁸	*11/2* ⁹	3¹⁰	4¹¹	5¹²	6¹³	7¹⁴	
	8¹⁵	9¹⁶	1¹⁷	*2* ¹⁸	3¹⁹	22/4 ²⁰	5²¹	
	6²²	7²³	8²⁴	9²⁵	1²⁶	*11/2* ²⁷	3²⁸	
	4²⁹	5³⁰						
1996 **O C T O B E R**			4¹	5²	6³	7⁴	8⁵	**YOUR PERSONAL MONTH** #3
	9⁶	1⁷	11/2 ⁸	*3* ⁹	4¹⁰	5¹¹	6¹²	
	7¹³	8¹⁴	9¹⁵	1¹⁶	2¹⁷	*3* ¹⁸	22/4 ¹⁹	
	5²⁰	6²¹	7²²	8²³	9²⁴	1²⁵	11/2 ²⁶	
	3 ²⁷	4²⁸	5²⁹	6³⁰	7³¹			

37

OCTOBER 1995

SUN	MON	TUES	WED	THURS	FRI	SAT
1	2	3	4	5	6	7
8	9	10	11	12	13	14
15	16	17	18	19	20	21
22	23	24	25	26	27	28
29	30	31				

YOUR PERSONAL MONTH:_____

NOVEMBER 1995

SUN	MON	TUES	WED	THURS	FRI	SAT
			1	2	3	4
5	6	7	8	9	10	11
12	13	14	15	16	17	18
19	20	21	22	23	24	25
26	27	28	29	30		

YOUR PERSONAL MONTH:_____

DECEMBER 1995

SUN	MON	TUES	WED	THURS	FRI	SAT
					1	2
3	4	5	6	7	8	9
10	11	12	13	14	15	16
17	18	19	20	21	22	23
24 / 31	25	26	27	28	29	30

YOUR PERSONAL MONTH:_____

JANUARY 1996

SUN	MON	TUES	WED	THURS	FRI	SAT
	1	2	3	4	5	6
7	8	9	10	11	12	13
14	15	16	17	18	19	20
21	22	23	24	25	26	27
28	29	30	31			

YOUR PERSONAL MONTH:_____

FEBRUARY 1996

SUN	MON	TUES	WED	THURS	FRI	SAT
				1	2	3
4	5	6	7	8	9	10
11	12	13	14	15	16	17
18	19	20	21	22	23	24
25	26	27	28	29		

YOUR PERSONAL MONTH:_____

MARCH 1996

SUN	MON	TUES	WED	THURS	FRI	SAT
					1	2
3	4	5	6	7	8	9
10	11	12	13	14	15	16
17	18	19	20	21	22	23
24 / 31	25	26	27	28	29	30

YOUR PERSONAL MONTH:_____

APRIL 1996

SUN	MON	TUES	WED	THURS	FRI	SAT
	1	2	3	4	5	6
7	8	9	10	11	12	13
14	15	16	17	18	19	20
21	22	23	24	25	26	27
28	29	30				

YOUR PERSONAL MONTH:_____

MAY 1996

SUN	MON	TUES	WED	THURS	FRI	SAT
			1	2	3	4
5	6	7	8	9	10	11
12	13	14	15	16	17	18
19	20	21	22	23	24	25
26	27	28	29	30	31	

YOUR PERSONAL MONTH:_____

JUNE 1996

SUN	MON	TUES	WED	THURS	FRI	SAT
						1
2	3	4	5	6	7	8
9	10	11	12	13	14	15
16	17	18	19	20	21	22
23 / 30	24	25	26	27	28	29

YOUR PERSONAL MONTH:_____

JULY 1996

SUN	MON	TUES	WED	THURS	FRI	SAT
	1	2	3	4	5	6
7	8	9	10	11	12	13
14	15	16	17	18	19	20
21	22	23	24	25	26	27
28	29	30	31			

YOUR PERSONAL MONTH:_____

AUGUST 1996

SUN	MON	TUES	WED	THURS	FRI	SAT
				1	2	3
4	5	6	7	8	9	10
11	12	13	14	15	16	17
18	19	20	21	22	23	24
25	26	27	28	29	30	31

YOUR PERSONAL MONTH:_____

SEPTEMBER 1996

SUN	MON	TUES	WED	THURS	FRI	SAT
1	2	3	4	5	6	7
8	9	10	11	12	13	14
15	16	17	18	19	20	21
22	23	24	25	26	27	28
29	30					

YOUR PERSONAL MONTH:_____

OCTOBER 1996

SUN	MON	TUES	WED	THURS	FRI	SAT
		1	2	3	4	5
6	7	8	9	10	11	12
13	14	15	16	17	18	19
20	21	22	23	24	25	26
27	28	29	30	31		

YOUR PERSONAL MONTH:_____

NOVEMBER 1996

SUN	MON	TUES	WED	THURS	FRI	SAT
					1	2
3	4	5	6	7	8	9
10	11	12	13	14	15	16
17	18	19	20	21	22	23
24	25	26	27	28	29	30

YOUR PERSONAL MONTH:_____

DECEMBER 1996

SUN	MON	TUES	WED	THURS	FRI	SAT
1	2	3	4	5	6	7
8	9	10	11	12	13	14
15	16	17	18	19	20	21
22	23	24	25	26	27	28
29	30	31				

YOUR PERSONAL MONTH:_____

Colors in Food

RED
apples
beets
red cabbage
cherries
radishes
raspberries
strawberries
tomatoes
watermelon
red meats

ORANGE
apricots
cantaloupes
carrots
mangoes
oranges
persimmons
pumpkins
nectarines
tangerines

YELLOW
bananas
corn
eggs
grapefruit
lemons
oils
peaches
pineapple
cheese
yams

GREEN
asparagus
artichokes
avocados
all lettuce
green
  vegetables
pears

BLUE
blueberries
loganberries
some grapes
blue plums

INDIGO
use the
blue and
violet
foods

VIOLET
blackberries
eggplant
dark grapes
purple plums
passion fruit
dulse

References

Your Days Are Numbered, by Florence Campbell.
De Vorss and Co., Marina del Rey, CA.

Numbers, the Complete Guide, by Mathew O. Goodman,
Newcastle Publishing, No. Hollywood, CA.

The Romance in Your Name, by Juno Jordan.
De Vorss and Co., Marina del Rey, CA.

Your Right Action Number, by Juno Jordan.
De Vorss and Co., Marina del Rey, CA.

Secrets of Numbers, by Johnson and Womback,
Samuel Weiser, Inc., New York, NY.